THAT YOU MIGHT HAVE LIFE

DAVID HAAS

That you might have

LIFE

12 SPIRITUAL PRACTICES
TO NURTURE YOUR CALL TO HOLINESS

**TWENTY-THIRD
PUBLICATIONS**
twentythirdpublications.com

Acknowledgments

All Scripture passages, unless otherwise noted, are taken from *The Common English Bible* (CEB), Copyright © 2011 Common English Bible, P.O. Box 801, 201 Eighth Avenue South, Nashville, TN, 37202-0801. Used with permission. All rights reserved.

The quote from Chapter 5, paragraph 40 of *The Dogmatic Constitution on the Church,* is adapted by Bill Huebsch, *Vatican II in Plain English: The Constitutions;* Ave Maria Press, Notre Dame, IN. Used with permission. All rights reserved.

All of the song-prayers that are recommended are by David Haas. They are available in various printed and recorded formats, and as individual MP3 downloads, from GIA Publications, Inc. 7404 South Mason Avenue, Chicago, IL 60638 (www.giamusic.com / 1-800-442-1358).

A complete digital download of all the song-prayers recommended in this book can be found at *giamusic.com/life*

TWENTY-THIRD PUBLICATIONS
A division of Bayard
One Montauk Avenue, Suite 200
New London, CT 06320
(860) 437-3012 or (800) 321-0411
www.twentythirdpublications.com

Cover Illustration: ©iStockphoto.com/Booblgum

ISBN: 978-1-62785-257-9
Library of Congress Control Number: 2016960021
Printed in the U.S.A.

A Division of Bayard, Inc.

Dedication

To Bill Huebsch—
master catechist and
guide for those aching
for holiness.

I am grateful to
Bill Huesbsch,
Fr. Michael Joncas,
Bonnie Faber,
Marty Haugen,
Sr. Kathleen Storms, SSND,
Valerie Sayre,
Fr. Richard Rohr, OFM,
Art Zannoni,
Fr. John Forliti,
Lori True,
Bishop Remi De Roo,
and Pearl Gervais for
their wisdom and
insights; and to
Dan Connors and
Trish Vanni
for their assistance.

CONTENTS

INTRODUCTION

All of us, whether we use "churchy" language or not, whether we are conscious of it or not, are aching for a more "spiritual" life. Everyone. Not just Catholics, but all Christians. And yes, this is true of Jews, Muslims, Hindus, and Buddhists, and even those who do not claim any specific kind of tribal connection. All are looking, searching, even aching for meaning.

Saint Pope John XXIII's call for an international ecumenical council (Vatican II) was in response to this ache. He was able to tap into the yearnings and groanings of a world in need of a God who could be closer and more engaged with our lives. He was able to see, as true visionaries do, that all of the people of God needed to be made aware that they actually *are* the people of God! And that *all* God's people—not just the ordained and religious—are worthy of the invitation to pursue holiness in their lives.

Yes...holiness.

And so, the Council, being led by the Spirit of God, proclaimed loud and clear this truth. Its teaching spoke the theme of the "universal call to holiness" boldly in *Lumen Gentium* (Christ is the Light of the Nations), otherwise known as The Dogmatic Constitution on the Church:

> We are called to holiness by Christ himself,
> who taught, in the words of St. Matthew,
> that we must be "perfect as God is perfect."

1

By transforming the activities and events
of everyday life into holy moments,
all the faithful grow in this perfection
and the world more and more resembles God's Reign.

So it is clear that everyone,
lay,
and ordained,
is called to be holy.

✦ CHAPTER 5, PARAGRAPH 40

This affirmation of the "universal call to holiness" is at the heart of what Vatican II was attempting to proclaim and announce: that everyone—and that means everyone—is called to holiness, to a sacred wholeness that comes in response to God's invitation given as the gift of grace. Grace is a free and unearned gift, a gift that is given to every living creature at the very moment of conception. This grace is constantly moving and stirring in our lives. God is active. God is not a noun. This God of ours is truly an action verb! God is here, engaged with all of us without distinction. As followers of Christ, we are charged with not only seeking and finding personal awareness of our own holiness; we are expected to help our sisters and brothers understand this reality, to celebrate it and ritualize it with honor and awe, and to live lives of discipleship that answer the promise of this holy invitation.

Yes, we are sinners, and so we may ask ourselves, how can we—how can I—possibly be holy? We often do not believe that we are worthy, that we do not live lives that deserve being called holy. So first off, we need to banish these self-loathing ways of seeing ourselves, because if worthiness were the criterion for holiness, none of us would be qualified to even begin the journey. Look at the people whom God called in the Hebrew Scriptures:

Moses—*he had a lisp. He could not speak well in complete sentences without stumbling. Aaron, his "press secretary," had to do all the talking. Yet Moses—not by talking but by his actions in faith—led the people to the promised land.*

Jeremiah—*too young*

David—*too short, and too promiscuous*

Job—*too bipolar*

Jonah—*too caught up with fish*

We could go on and on. Let's look at some of the characters in the New Testament:

Mary—*a young teenager having a child outside of marriage*

John the Baptist—*a hippie who wore camel's hair and ate bugs*

Matthew—*tax collector (are you kidding?!)*

Mary Magdalene and the Samaritan Woman—*too female*

Paul—*in his early years worthy of today's label of "terrorist"*

And then we have *all* of the twelve apostles as examples, especially Peter. Peter never really "gets it." Jesus wants to wash feet; Peter says no way. Jesus is taking a nap when the storm brews up on the boat; Peter gets an anxiety attack and cannot move. Jesus presents himself transfigured with Elijah and Moses, providing a glimpse of God's reign; Peter gets selfish and wants to set up camp. Jesus freely offers himself to be handcuffed and arrested; Peter gets visions of grandeur and, wanting to be the hero, slices off the ear of one of the high priest's servants. Jesus is being tried and scourged and humiliated; Peter denies even knowing who Jesus is.

Despite all of this, the Church recognizes Peter as the first pope.

Rock of the Church. Actually, he is more of a quivering bowl of mush, yes?

And yet all of these characters (and many more, too many to begin to name) were called to the path of holiness. Who does God call? All of us. The flawed. The wounded. The sinful. Often, the screw-ups of society.

It is not that God did not do good market research in hiring witnesses for the Reign of God. It is the fact that God does not operate under our templates for doing things. It is not that these characters, these saints, were perfect and loving; it is because *God* was, and *is still*, perfect and loving. God is the meeting point of the holiness journey. Consider Peter again for a moment. In a parallel to denying who Jesus was three times, when Jesus asks Peter after the resurrection the ultimate question of holiness, Peter responds: "Yes, Lord, you know I love you." The journey toward holiness moved forward for Peter. The journey moves forward for each of us. All of us.

This holiness is a paschal journey. It is a journey of dying to ourselves and giving ourselves over totally to God's pattern and definition of what love really is. Holiness is where and when we prune ourselves, peeling back the coverings and outer skins of the things that keep us away from God's way.

When we do this, the way to holiness opens us up to let go of our fear, to empty ourselves, place ourselves at the back of the line, and pull others to sit in front. Then, we talk less and serve more. Holiness is when we become more "other" centered in everything, when the poor—both the materially and spiritually poor—become one with us. Holiness is when the story of Jesus—his life, his deeds, his death, and the blazing light of his rising—becomes real for *us,* in *our* lives, in *our* deeds, and yes, in *our* dying and rising.

Here is the bottom line: God loves us. There is absolutely nothing we can do about that. There is nothing that we can do that can push that love away. So we are invited to stop fighting and instead accept and celebrate this love. We are invited to join the movement of this holy journey, allowing this love to percolate and move and have its way with us. Surrendering to this invitation is the starting block of the lifetime adventure of holiness.

Walking the road and riding the roller-coaster of moving toward holiness is a most daunting task. We need touchstones, patterns, strategies, and practices that help make the lanes a bit wider for us to travel on. With this booklet, I hope that all of you—whether you do so individually or in a small group of some kind (which is ideal, but not required)—can find ways to more authentically "put on Christ" and have Christ be not just the Jesus of history that we admire and adore but a living presence that we can own and embrace. By doing this, we can come closer to the goal of being the "light of the nations," having life, and having it to the full. You know...holiness.

How to use this book

There is no one way to use this book. You need to decide what works best for you. You can use it as your own personal inventory guide or journal, as a spiritual "12-step" journey (akin to, but different in many ways, to the twelve steps that anchor those who are on the lifelong road of recovery). There is no specific or correct "order" in which to meditate and reflect on these spiritual practices, and they are not presented here in any "scope-and-sequence" kind of template. You can change the order, you can make them a part of a personal retreat for yourself, or you can use them as a series of touchstones that you visit off and on—perhaps during the season of Lent, or any time that renewal is calling you.

Ideally, this would be a good journey to make with a small faith-sharing group, or with a group of friends—those who know you well and are on a similar spiritual search in their own lives. There are questions at the end of each reflection (each practice) for your group discussion or for your own meditation and prayer. There is space to take notes and jot reflections of your own.

Finally, each section ends with what I call a choice of "song-prayers," liturgical pieces that can help you reflect even more deeply and maybe even sing along. My hope is that this will deepen the "sinking in" of each practice. Music has that power. Words by themselves are one thing. But when we can sing and feel our hearts vibrating when we sing along, the words and the prayer can cut through more deeply. Conversion may be waiting just around the corner.

In the end, I hope you'll make this booklet work for you as one path of ongoing reflection. I hope you'll find in its suggestions the courage to move forward on your own path of holiness toward sacred "wholeness." It is here for you, in the words of Jesus, "that you might have life." ◆ D H

SUGGESTED SONG-PRAYER
TO BEGIN THE JOURNEY

That You Might Have Life
DAVID HAAS, GIA PUBLICATIONS
Digital MP3 Download available
from www.giamusic.com: X-80310

ONE

Awaken your spiritual practices

Pursue the Lord. • **1 CHRONICLES 16:11A**

You are close, Lord, to all who call on you. • **PSALM 145:18A**, *The Grail*

Pray continually...Don't suppress the Spirit. Don't brush off Spirit-inspired messages, but examine everything carefully and hang on to what is good. • **1 THESSALONIANS 5:17, 19–21**

Living a spiritually mature life requires listening to God's voice within and among us. • **HENRI NOUWEN**, *Discernment*

Every human person, whether conscious of it or not, inherently desires to live life on a deeper level. We all have an inner hope that we can move from living a "worry-filled" life to more of a "spiritual" life, whatever that may mean for us.

There is not a "one-size-fits-all" prescription for achieving this. All of us possess a unique spiritual DNA, so to speak, a distinct kind of hard-wiring that is unique to each and every one of us. Each of us has a distinct path by which we somehow access and nurture the sacred in our lives. This is the path toward holiness. It's a path, not an "arrival." True holiness and wholeness are not about arriving at a final destination, and are certainly not about "getting there," like a graduation prize. True holiness and wholeness are found in the path, in the process, in the pilgrimage.

What does it mean to live the spiritual life? What is spirituality? What is our vocation in living a God-centered life existence?

To speak plainly, let us say that to live the spiritual life is this: to walk in the full brilliance of the light of God, knowing with full surrender that God is God and we are not. To live wholly and holy is to accept and celebrate the glorious truth that God is in charge. Everything else that follows is merely the way in which this blessed truth is affirmed and awakened. Living the life of prayer, to "pray continually," is to recognize that every breath that we take is the breathing in and out of God's presence—when we are conscious of it and when we are *not* conscious of it (which may be most of the time!).

This sacred awakening is at the very heart of the familiar sacramental understanding of the world that most of us have grown up with, of how we encounter and celebrate the holy in our lives. As Catholics, we believe that all of creation is holy. For most of us, our primary filter (and for some of us, it has been the only filter) for hearing about God, praying to God, and growing in our faith in God has been the liturgy.

However, liturgy is *not* where faith is actually "activated" most of the time. This activation of our faith happens usually in the "everydayness" of life. It happens in the ordinary, sometimes dull and, yes, sometimes extraordinary things and happenstances of life. To speak more theologically, the liturgy is the *celebration* of that activation. It is the place where that activation is nurtured, celebrated, reveled in, and expanded so it can explode forth from our lives *after* the specific liturgical celebration is over. It is the time when we gather together with other pilgrims and place this ongoing expansion before the tables of the word and the shared meal, and the light blazes even more brilliantly. It is not "magic," but it is in so many ways truly magical in leading us to our ultimate mission—discipleship.

We need to remember that each of the seven sacraments and every liturgical celebration is an event in which we encounter God's transformative grace. Some of these moments are singular; for example, we are only baptized once. Others happen again and again, such as the Eucharist. Our liturgical and sacramental life grounds us spiritually.

Why must we repeat some of these actions over and over? Because, sadly, we keep forgetting. We keep forgetting about God's presence and our ongoing and eternal call to be living witnesses of God's love. We need these spiritual, communal, and ritual reminders to keep us connected to our primary vocation as sons and daughters of God who are called by Christ. And our call is to be ongoing and dedicated witnesses of God's love.

Our liturgical and sacramental lives are centered in community, as sisters and brothers. We are not called to live in isolation but with each other. Even though our liturgical celebrations may not always be exciting, inspiring, or particularly "relevant" in the actual moment, they still discipline us to be attentive and loyal to the inherent richness of our faith and to have our hearts opened. As a Catholic, I would suggest that they should be our central spiritual practices—particularly Eucharist, which we profess as the source and summit of the Christian life.

Still, there are other practices that we do together (and yes, alone) that can nurture and deepen our holiness. They vary for each of us. Some of us find the richness in having a spiritual director, or making an annual individual retreat. Some of us have found great awakenings to our own holiness in the practices of other liturgical forms of prayer, such as Taizé prayer or praying the Liturgy of the Hours. Others have discovered meditation/contemplation, or other devotions like praying the Rosary, praying the Stations of the Cross, or praying with holy icons.

Many have found great spiritual growth in participating in a

Bible-study or prayer group, or by engaging in spiritual reading and reflection. Being centered in God's word is critical and cannot be emphasized enough. Scripture! Scripture! Scripture! God's word needs to stop being the stranger that is has been for so many. Reflection and study—reading at least a short passage each day, or keeping some of our favorite Bible verses close to our heart—needs to be our medallion of strength for this spiritual pilgrimage.

So, a common rhythm of liturgy and the sacraments is important. These are the practices through which together we become the body of Christ. And yes, some form of nurturing our journey as individual members of the body—some blend of solitude/meditation/contemplation and other practices that nurture our hearts—is important too, because we bring those spiritual blessings back to the greater body. There is not one recipe that will feed all. Each of us has to figure out and discern what mix of practices is filling. But what is commonly critical for all of us is that we engage in some path of holy conversation with God. It is in that conversation that we come closer to ourselves and our vocation to be servants of the amazing love of God.

■ PROCESS

Questions for Reflection and Action
FOR INDIVIDUAL AND GROUP REFLECTION

What kind of spiritual practices are a regular part of my life?

How are they life-giving?

How can I be more attentive to nurturing holy conversations?

What new spiritual practice might I want to pursue?

Song-Prayers

Increase Our Faith
DAVID HAAS, GIA PUBLICATIONS
*Digital Mp3 Download available
from www.giamusic.com: X-80608*

Without Seeing You
DAVID HAAS, GIA PUBLICATIONS
*Digital MP3 Download available
from www.giamusic.com: X-80332*

TWO

Honor your body; keep moving

Don't you know that your body is a temple of the Holy Spirit who is in you?....Honor God with your body. • 1 CORINTHIANS 6:19A, 20B

We are God's accomplishment. • EPHESIANS 2:10

Dear friend, I'm praying that all is well with you and that you enjoy good health in the same way that you prosper spiritually. • 3 JOHN 2

My body is much more than a mortal instrument of pleasure and gain. It is a home where God wants to manifest the fullness of the divine glory.
• HENRI NOUWEN, *The Road to Daybreak*

In one of the many boxes of old photographs that I have, there is a photo of me holding a "SlimFast" shake in one hand and a juicy jelly donut in the other. For a few moments of twisted logic, I thought that drinking a sip of the shake after biting into the donut would somehow balance out the poison that I was chewing on. I know, you are laughing.

Diet and nutrition are a struggle for most of us in the U.S. As for me, I have always liked my meat and potatoes. I'm a carnivore at heart. I have never liked fruits and vegetables. I love my comfort food!

And then there is the challenge of exercise. When we were younger, we naturally "moved" more. Activity was more inherent and woven into our lives. In school we were involved in activities where exercise was not always conscious but part of our daily routines. We walked all the time. We just moved more. Now I sit at my desk, sit at the piano, or sit at the many meetings that I have to attend for hours and hours. Not a lot of moving.

When I was much younger these things just did not matter much to me. For the early years of my adult life, just like when I was a boy, I had a very high metabolism, and I was pretty skinny. That self-image, and the ways of behaving that accompanied it, were locked into my psyche. To this day, my brain wants to think that way. As the years have gone by, I've struggled with the ongoing challenge of weight gain. The result has been that I don't have the same energy that I used to have.

Not too many years ago, I was with a couple of friends who were struggling with the same change of reality. We walked by a man who was in impeccable shape—he obviously worked out and exercised regularly and ate well. His body was svelte and well sculpted. After we walked by, one of my friends said: "He treats his body like a temple, and we treat ours like low-income housing projects."

As we move through our lives, these realities are hard to face. But all of us need to reflect on how we take care of our bodies in terms of food and exercise. If we don't have healthy practices, when stress and anxiety set in, we sit and we stew, spiraling downward. Then we freeze. The result is that the stress and anxiety keep climbing.

While many persons in our lives will try to tell us that there is one way, one program to follow, there just isn't. What is true, though, is that something most certainly may need to change, not only in our concrete strategies but in the way we look at ourselves—which often doesn't mirror the way that God looks at and sees us.

God wants good things for us, and our faith in this God who loves us more than we can imagine rests in adjusting our thinking. Faith is not the result of successful solutions that overcome obstacles. Rather, our faith is deeply locked into this gracious God, this most blessed glance that God has fixed on us. If we can really let that glance from God take us over, then we can come to face and express our fears and worries "all the way through."

As we approach and struggle with the issues of better diet and more regular exercise, we need to drink in this mantra: "God wants good things for me." If we can internalize this truth, then we can muster up the courage to find the exercise regimen and food plan that makes the most sense for us. Yes, we need to honor the temple that is our body. Yes, we need to keep moving. But we need to discover ways where we can make better choices and meet the struggle without blame, shame, or guilt. Seeing ourselves as God's beloved and holy ones can help us make these transformational shifts. It will, gradually over a period of time, result in not just losing weight or feeling more energized physically, but in truly being able to look in the mirror and celebrate that we most certainly are God's work of art, God's "accomplishment."

■ PROCESS

Questions for Reflection and Action
For individual and group reflection

What keeps me from implementing a plan for my bodily health?

What paralyzes me and keeps me from making a change?

What one small step can I make right now, for the better?

To whom can I go to receive support for this new adventure?

Song-Prayer

You Are God's Work of Art
DAVID HAAS, GIA PUBLICATIONS
*Digital MP3 Download available
from www.giamusic.com: X-80341*

THREE

Remember that you are the beloved

God is present to you; God will create calm with love for you;
God will rejoice in you, singing and rejoicing!
• **ZEPHANIAH 3: 17. PARAPHRASE BY DH**

I am convinced that nothing can separate us from God's love. • **ROMANS 8:38A**

God cares for you. • **I PETER 5:7B. PARAPHRASE BY DH**

Self-rejection is the greatest enemy of the spiritual life because
it contradicts the sacred voice that calls us the "Beloved."
Being the Beloved expresses the core truth of our existence.
HENRI NOUWEN, *Life of the Beloved: Spiritual Living in a Secular World*

There are so many outside voices that penetrate our psychological and spiritual membranes. They stir all kinds of things up inside of us and affect our personal sense of identity.

I was highly sensitive as a young boy (I still am!). I remember the refrain that so many recommended I throw back at those who taunted me: "Sticks and bones will break my bones, but words will never hurt me." Well, that did not work for me at all. The words *did* hurt. The words *did* matter.

While I remember getting beat up on the playground and at the bus stop when I was little, I have to say that the taunting and cruel "words" did more damage (and still linger today) than the physical bruises that healed much more quickly. Verbal abuse cuts to the core for us. These poisons do more than just inform our self-talk. Such words and the long- and short-term memories of such words actually shape our sense of ourselves.

We each have a deep need to be loved, to feel loved. For some of us, this ache is so deep that it becomes the criterion for how and what we think about ourselves. But this lens—one that looks at us from the outside in—is very distorted, even when the feedback is positive. That's because what others think of us, or their opinions about what we do, do not even come close to defining who we are. I've come to see that when I put "wanting you to like me" ahead of the *me* that God wants me to be and has created me to be, I am asking for trouble.

The source of our sense of who we are and how we think and talk to ourselves needs to be placed back into the heart and mind of God. Our traits, our personality types, our unique moods, skills, gifts, and abilities, as well as the labels that others want to place upon us (both positive and negative), are not the ultimate definition of who we each are.

We can recognize this in the fact that one day in the future, sometimes sooner than we can predict, these "outer" things will drift away. For some of us, they will be actually "taken away," drastically, in ways that seem to be so cruelly unfair. None of these things is "forever." None of them are eternal. They are temporary, fleeting, and finite. And I'd suggest that in the end they do not matter.

When we come to grips with this, what do we do? Like the choreographer says to those auditioning to make the "cut" in the Broadway musical *A Chorus Line*, "What do you do when you can't dance anymore?" What do we do when we cannot dance anymore, teach anymore, make or build things anymore, play the piano or sing anymore? What do we do when we can no longer lead and supervise budgets and employees, when we can no longer run, or analyze, or do whatever it is that we "do"?

We draw ourselves back to our deeper identity, an identity beyond what we have done or have had. We are the beloved of God, God's adopted daughters and sons. Regardless of what we have achieved, or hope to achieve, because we are God's, we have already *arrived*.

Each of us needs to dig deep and celebrate who we are—not what we *do*—and find the courage to recognize that we are wonderful just as we are. We are so very special, so very precious indeed. No one person, no force of circumstances, no outside influences can ever take that away. God is so over-the-top thrilled with who we are, simply because we are here, alive. To deny this corrective "version" of who we are is to deny the glory of God. We are, as St. Paul proclaims over and over again, alive "in Christ." Our baptism celebrates this. We are much more than just OK. We are so very full of the divine light and presence of God.

You and I are as much a child of God as Jesus was and is. Listen to that again. We are as much a child of God as Jesus. Whether or not we can accept this will play a large part in whether or not we can move forward in wholeness and holiness. We are *not* (as many who call themselves Christian would have us believe) pitiful, sick sinners.

Now, do we often live and choose to live in pitiful ways? Yes, we do. Are we broken people who are in need of a physician? Yes, we are. Are we all sinners, or better put—are we wounded people who often make tragic mistakes? Yes, again. But these are what Paul would call "momentary afflictions," and they do not define our identity—they are *not* what and who we are. When God calls upon us to "choose life," *this* is what that call is asking of us: we are called to transform and redirect our thinking about ourselves. The voices that we too often choose to listen to, both from others and from ourselves, are, sadly, the voices of bitterness, anger, and self-loathing. These voices are not of God.

So our mantras and voices need to announce to ourselves that we are as much of a child of God as Jesus is. Christ is present in us. In fact, we are Christ.

We need to exorcise the self-talk that pulls us into not only poor self-esteem but, at its most poisonous, our self-loathing. Time to stop the sentence of believing that we have to do restitution. No more paying the price for things that God has never asked us to pay for. We are God's beloved children. God wants the best for us, but do *we*?

We are being invited—actually commanded—to look in the mirror and see this light. It is not arrogant to do so, nor is it elitist. Because this "chosen-ness" that we revel in always recognizes that this same "chosen-ness" dwells in every other person as well. That is right. We do not earn it or "deserve" it or are "awarded" it so that this status puts us above others. To be "in Christ" is to be named as God's choice. This means that there is nothing we can do, or anything that others can do, that can separate us from this amazing, outpouring love of God. That is right. There is nothing too disgusting, too heinous, too horrific, too "sinful" that will push God away. It is not possible for God to be pushed away, no matter how awful we may see ourselves to be. All we have to do is to read again the story of the prodigal son to know that this is true. Not only is God not turning away from us, but like the loving father in that story, God is running toward us! Yes, even when we feel we are our worst selves!

We need to just stop it: stop the negative self-talk that is the ultimate defiance of God's astonishingly lavish love for us. My God, we are so wonderful! My God, our sisters and brothers— yes, even those who drive us crazy, or whom we see as "enemy"— are wonderful as well.

So let us begin to lighten up on ourselves and find new and holy ways to see ourselves and talk to ourselves the way that God sees and speaks to us—with so much love. And let us give thanks.

◼ PROCESS

Questions for Reflection and Action
FOR INDIVIDUAL AND GROUP REFLECTION

*Who and what were the voices from my past that bruised,
and may still continue to bruise, my self-esteem?*

---

*What are some loving things that I need to say to myself to heal those
wounds?*

---

*What concrete ways can I take to change old thinking, to welcome in
God's voice and view of who I am?*

---

*What might be the mantras or slogans or voices that I can use to
replace the old and destructive ones?*

Song-Prayers

The Beloved of God
DAVID HAAS, GIA PUBLICATIONS
Digital MP3 Download available from www.giamusic.com: X-9036CD01

Who Calls You By Name
DAVID HAAS, GIA PUBLICATIONS
Digital MP3 Download available from www.giamusic.com: X-73107

FOUR

Always be in discernment

Don't be conformed to the patterns of this world, but be transformed by the renewing of your minds so that you can figure out what God's will is—what is good and pleasing and mature. • **ROMANS 12:2**

This is my prayer: that your love might become even more and more rich with knowledge and all kinds of insight. • **PHILIPPIANS 1:9**

We haven't stopped praying for you and asking for you to be filled with the knowledge of God's will, with all wisdom and spiritual understanding. We're praying this so that you can live lives that are worthy of the Lord...
• **COLOSSIANS 1:9–10A**

Anyone who needs wisdom should ask God, whose very nature is to give to everyone without a second thought...Wisdom will certainly be given to those who ask. Whoever asks shouldn't hesitate. They should ask in faith... • **JAMES 1:5–6A**

The purpose of discernment is to know God's will, that is, to find, accept, and affirm the unique way in which God's love is manifest in our life... Discernment reveals new priorities, directions, and gifts from God. We come to realize that what previously seemed so important for our lives, loses its power over us. • **HENRI NOUWEN,** *Discernment*

The ongoing goal of any spiritual practice or journey is to "awaken." Our patterns of prayer and holy growth are to awaken, ignite, and provide a "lift off" to our most sacred and vulnerable desires.

This is the path of prayerful discernment. This is the map that we study so that we can listen more attentively to God's voice and, as a result, make choices in light of what that voice is saying. This is a central truth about what prayer is. Prayer is not so much asking for specific things in the hope that things will go "our way" according to our limited understanding. No, the prayer of discernment is an exercise and discipline of *listening*. Listening to what God is trying to say to us.

When other people are described as being "prayerful people," it usually means that they are both attentive and mindful. To be prayer-filled in this way is to have a spiritual antenna up and running. Open and receptive in this way, the well can stay full—but full of our vulnerable self, full of God being so very present to this hidden, most tender, and vulnerable self.

Discernment is when we listen to God and pay attention to God's presence in our inner life of work and prayer. It happens when we can observe the nudges that are coming our way from God, often through the observations and nudges from our spiritual friends and guides. These companions prompt us in a particular direction, often providing templates for making new and transformative choices.

Discernment means to "see rightly." The final destination is not a place, but a daily falling into God's embrace. Such discernment is daily and ongoing and can help us see whether our choices are being lived out for ourselves only or lived out for the glory of God. Discernment is the process in which we look at life and things through the eyes of God, not our own eyes. When we move in the direction and knowledge of the Holy One who accompanies us on the journey, then the cause of wholeness and holiness have a good beginning and an ongoing compass.

Another important aspect of this is to remember that discernment is not linear. We are very focused in other aspects of our lives on "goals and objectives." This approach doesn't work for achieving spiritual wisdom and contentment. The spiritual life can be very erratic and unpredictable. It requires an ongoing discipline and commitment to listen well and attentively. It asks that we listen with eagerness to the small, gentle, and quiet voices that are trying to break through in the midst of a crazy, rushed, over-committed, and very "loud" world.

Discernment asks us to find a new set of spiritual glasses that can help us see and navigate the subtle and more hidden signs in our daily lives. Discernment may not bring us to a one-time final destination where all of our decisions and concerns suddenly come together in great clarity. While ordinary and important decisions and new chapters take place in the midst of our discernment journey—such as deciding whether or not to take on a new job or career, with whom I should spend the rest of my life, or where I should move to—these are not, in and of themselves, the landing point of discernment. In fact, there is no final landing point at all in living the spiritual life and embracing holiness.

Discernment is a lifelong pilgrimage where we keep remembering who God is. It is one where we look deeply and reflectively at who we are, staying open to what the Spirit of God is trying to say to us and where it may be leading us. It is about listening to and taking part in a deeper and more sustaining sound—the sound of God walking with us in every aspect of our lives. It is not about learning more; it is about *experiencing* more and letting God be at the center of those experiences, to "live lives that are worthy of the Lord" (Colossians 1:10).

If we embark on the journey of discernment, we have to realize that at times it will be frustrating and unnerving. It may often be filled with more questions than answers. It is a daily practice. Actually it is even more than that. It is not living "one day at a time" but living "one moment at a time."

But we need to be open to the comfort and assurance that we do not do so alone. God is with us, whether we recognize that presence or not. God comes to us in the ordinary and "everyday-ness" of our lives. Knowing this, our suffering is transformed from something that must be held at bay into a sojourn that recognizes that Christ is present and attentive to our pain. This journey is one where we find new courage, hope, and trust in the guiding lights that are greater than our own particular spiritual flashlight. We become able to trust enough to let go and let a new freedom come over us and dwell within us—it is truly "living in the Spirit."

Where can discernment lead us? It is different for each of us, but we can hope and expect some basic things to begin to come true. We can begin to realize, wisely, that our lives need not be so frantic and full of chaos. We can bring about patterns of living that lead to less anxiety. We can avoid fear-driven decisions and destructive habits. We can approach things that are unknown and scary with a greater sense of courage. Solitude can be less threatening; we can begin to develop and really enjoy just being with ourselves—even celebrating a new relationship with ourselves. Paradox and ambiguity begin to be things not to be feared but realities to embrace. We can find a new awareness of ourselves and others that will open up doors of dialogue where judgment and blame have deterred us.

Discernment is about choosing new ways of living by letting God give the direction. Discernment begins, develops, and is nurtured by our decision to seek God and to listen to God.

■ PROCESS

Questions for Reflection and Action
FOR INDIVIDUAL AND GROUP REFLECTION

How do I want to be seen by God?

Who are the "spiritual friends" in my world in whom I place my trust, whom I want to know me well, and who can make this walk with me?

What are the ways in which I listen to God?

What are some new practices that I can embrace to move forward in my discernment journey?

Song-Prayers

Do Not Let Your Hearts Be Troubled
DAVID HAAS, GIA PUBLICATIONS
*Digital MP3 Download available
from www.giamusic.com: X-80314*

My Soul Waits for God
DAVID HAAS, GIA PUBLICATIONS
*Digital MP3 Download available
from www.giamusic.com: X-82212*

FIVE

Find a mantra; use it often

Let the words of my mouth and the meditations of my heart be pleasing to you. • **PSALM 19:14A**

Be still, and know that I am God. • **PSALM 46:10, NRSV**

Pray continually. • **1 THESSALONIANS 5:17**

Mantra is a phrase that is designed to free the mind.
• **ROBIN SHARMA,** *The Monk Who Sold his Ferrari*

In the morning, stand up, stretch, find a mantra, pray, breathe, and be grateful for the day. Speak an affirmation out loud: "I am a child of God. God, guide my steps."

There are times when we wake up in the morning and wonder if God really does have a plan for us. Or perhaps the message is that we have to keep on the same course that we have been moving in for the remainder of our days. Such thoughts can sadden us and even pull us into depression, because we so desperately want to change, to have things be different, to cope in healthier ways than we presently do, to release some of the anxiety and stress that can cripple us. We can feel trapped by the present state of affairs.

We ache to find ways to focus and talk better to ourselves. We need a method, a template at times, that reminds us there is a "plan," a direction, and a compass than can help us move forward and not remain frozen.

Mantras are a way. They are centering reminders that we are not alone, that God is with us. They also help us to be present to ourselves in the moment, in the midst of our fears and uncertainty.

Mantras can clarify that we are *not* what we do or what other people say we should be. They can "talk us down" from anxiety and our false ways of seeing a situation. Our vocation is *always* to be a witness of God's love. Nothing else really matters. Mantras can calm us down to remember this, to invest in what is primary once again. Each time we utter them it is as if we are doing so for the very first time. A mantra like "I am a witness of God's love" can be a new start to a new challenge, a new race, a new journey or pilgrimage that greets us as we embark on a new day.

Mantras are centered in our breath. As we listen to our breath, we become aware that the very "in and out" of our breath is the presence of God with and in us. To stay alive, we need to keep breathing. We are being asked to simply *enjoy* that for a while. After basking in that enjoyment, we can then attach a word or a phrase that rides on our breath. We focus not so much on the cognitive recognition or definitions of the words, but on the calming down and centering that these breath-centered words can provide.

There, in the midst of timeless space, it is possible that we will hear a voice that is speaking lovingly to us, and we can trust in this guidance that is coming our way. Allowing ourselves to be drawn into such intentional stillness will probably not provide clear-cut, rational answers, but it can point us in a particular direction. It can allow us to hear the voice of God, which has been there, is there now, and will always be speaking to us.

By doing this, we let God's heart speak to our heart. This is a prayer, yes, but not a prayer that is asking for things, one where we do the "talking." No, this is prayer when we are truly "listening" to what God is trying to say to us.

Here are some examples of some mantras that we can use. These may open a door for us to discover some refrains of our own:

"God, I thank you that last night was not my last night."

"There is one thing I ask of the Lord" (breathe in),
"to live in the house of the Lord" (breathe out).

"God's cause is the only concern of our hearts."

"Draw near to God and God will draw near to you." • JAMES 4:8, NRSV

"God is well pleased with me."

A mantra (or more than one—you can be greedy about this!) really can be our friend, our rock, something that provides footing when it feels like we are sinking into the quicksand. Find a mantra. Have it become a lifeline. Help it to center your heart, your breathing, your mind on God. And in doing so, you have an opportunity to come back to yourself.

■ PROCESS

Questions for Reflection and Action
FOR INDIVIDUAL AND GROUP REFLECTION

When are the times when I need to draw on something to pull me back to the center?

_____

_____

What short Scripture passages or other slogans or refrains provide strength and calm me?

_____

_____

Song-Prayers

You Are Always Present
DAVID HAAS, GIA PUBLICATIONS
Digital MP3 Download available from www.giamusic.com: X-82203

Only You
DAVID HAAS, GIA PUBLICATIONS
Digital MP3 Download available from www.giamusic.com: X-94403

God's Cause
DAVID HAAS, GIA PUBLICATIONS
Digital MP3 Download available from www.giamusic.com: X-71633

SIX

Examine your relationships

Walk with wise people and become wise; befriend fools and get in trouble.
• **PROVERBS 13:20**

You didn't receive a spirit of slavery to lead you back again into fear,
but you received a Spirit that shows you are adopted as his children...
If God is for us, who is against us? • **ROMANS 8:15, 31B**

Accept each other with love, and make an effort to preserve the unity
of the Spirit with the peace that ties you together. • **EPHESIANS 4:2B–3**

It is very hard for love not to become possessive because our hearts look
for perfect love and no human being is capable of that. Only God can offer
perfect love. Therefore, the art of loving includes the art of giving one
another space. When we invade one another's space and do not allow
the other to be his or her own free person, we cause great suffering in our
relationships. But when we give another space to move and share our gifts,
true intimacy becomes possible.
• **HENRI NOUWEN**, *Bread for the Journey*

Relationships are wonderful blessings, but they are also challenging, difficult, and at times very disappointing in the deep hurt they cause. Often we are hurt because we have forgotten that, just like us, other people are not perfect.

Most of us have primary and committed relationships with a spouse or partner, parents, children, and other family members. Some of us do not. Regardless, it might be safe to say that we operate with three circles or "zones" of relationships, all revolving back and forth, not in any clean or efficient flow. First are those who love us unconditionally and who delight in everything we do and are. Second are those who love us and yet also speak the truth to us—they offer affirmation and support, but they also challenge and call us to be better. And finally, there are our troubled relationships, those that are often unpredictable, volatile, and sometimes even toxic.

Now, laying down your life for your friends is one thing (John 15:13), but sometimes we need to ask: When we are drowning and continually bruised by certain relationships, are these people truly our friends? They may not necessarily be our enemies, nor should we foster having enemies in our lives. Everyone is a child of God. But we perhaps need to be courageous enough to recognize that some people who constantly trigger suffering for us or that push us—whether it be intentional or not—toward our ongoing self-loathing may not really be our friends.

Let's back up a few steps here. As Christians, we need to always remember that when we enter into any kind of relationship, we have to accept and take on a deep willingness to forgive over and over again. This is what it really means when we want Christ to be at the heart of our relationships. To put Christ at the center of our relationships, ironically, is to know and believe at the very start that the other person, no matter how wonderful they may be—is not Christ. When we grapple with relationships that are not "healthy," we may have to reconsider whether or not we can stay. Sometimes this is short term—like having to walk away from a particular conversation. Perhaps some space is needed to heal the distress and cool down the temperature. At other times, it is more long-term: We may have to discern whether or not this relationship is life-giving any more.

This is so hard and so very painful. When relationships have to change, the process can range from difficult to excruciating. We want things to be like they were before with the other person; we ache to have "it back" like it once was. But relationships evolve. Many of them, probably most of them, are not forever. It does not mean that they are bad or that they were wrong at one point. It just means that they—and the people in them—are not static.

When we examine a relationship that is going through what seems to be a long period of volatility and stress, we can ask: "Is this relationship positive more often than not?" This is not to let ourselves off the hook, because we ourselves need to take a hard look at our own behavior, choices, and ways of operating with our relationships. But when a hurtful comment or action from another person comes our way and shatters us to our core, we need to realize that this is less often about us than it is about the person who is throwing the poison dart. Sometimes the lashing out toward us happens in "nanoseconds" before we can find a filter to reflect, and then our first reaction is to lash back, to throw our own poison darts or, worse yet, try to engage with the other person to either defend ourselves or to try to negotiate with them to change their minds about what they are angry at us about. In my experience this almost never works.

When these things happen, we need to choose differently, if we can. When such comments or actions come at us from someone else, can we try to take on a more self-caring response? When a painful attack, often verbal, comes our way, can we internally or externally say, "ouch!" and then simply walk away? When we try to stay in such a conflicted situation, it more often than not makes things worse, and things spiral downward into a well of negative and shaming behavior that tries to "one-up" (or "one-down") the other person. Then the poison becomes more potent, more hurtful, more destructive. Then it becomes returning evil with evil.

Sometimes we need to *not* respond. Playing "defense attorney" most of the time just deepens the hurt and breaks our hearts even more. Again, this is so very hard to do. When I experience cruelty from someone, I need to remember that it is about their pain. It is the very same case when I myself am hurtful or cruel to others. It is about ME, about MY pain, MY jealousy...MY stuff.

To live "in Christ" means to try with all of the energy that we can muster to respond differently in such situations. When others are hurtful, our response needs to be graceful, compassionate, and loving. This can certainly sound very naïve and unrealistic. But there is no avoiding it—this is the way of Christ.

But it does *not* mean that we are to sacrifice ourselves and our emotional, mental, and spiritual health—especially when we do try to respond in a graceful, loving, and compassionate way and it seems to only result in more shame and hurt coming our way. These are signs that we may need to very seriously consider whether or not we can continue to remain in the situation.

When we "walk away," it may be just for a while, while things cool down and until reconciliation and restoration can occur. Or maybe for much longer. Or maybe—if the particular relationship seems to continue to fester and become more and more destructive over a period of time—it needs to end. Remember—and this is painful to accept—not every relationship is intended to last forever—especially when the relationship is making us feel more and more inadequate, or worse, as though we are bad people. We are not. Each of us is a child of God—a son or a daughter of the Lord. Not only do we not deserve to feel as though we are bad or useless or loathsome, to take this on is to defy God's way of seeing us as the beloved, as a work of art, as a precious creation.

We need to ask questions of such relationships and situations. "Is this person pushing up against who I really am, at the very core of my personhood and sense of who I am in the eyes of God?" "Am I spending the majority of my time explaining and defending myself?" It's not that we are perfect. We have probably made some mistakes and acted in ways that have caused hurt for the person who is throwing the arrows at us. But if we are being made to feel as though we are the sole blame for the other's problem, if the other person refuses adamantly to face their part in the toxic dance, if the other person does not believe that they have any work to do in the healing of the relationship and that everything has to change from our end alone, then something has to change. We all deserve a certain portion of forgiveness. We all deserve not to be totally defined by our worst moments and actions. True friendship—and this is why friendship is not an easy enterprise—works to forgive and chooses, even when we are hurting, to see the presence of God in the other and to allow that particular image to rise above everything else.

We cannot feel awful about ourselves without our own consent. When we stay in relationships and environments that are toxic, we are giving ourselves over to the sad state of another person's psychological and spiritual darkness. These are the "principalities and powers" that Paul speaks about and that God's love for us conquers and rises above and restores.

When we choose to stay in relationships, the loving and compassionate response, while so very difficult, is the path that we pray we have the strength to take. When we are being criticized and beaten down, we need to respond to the other person, either out loud or from the silence of our hearts: "You have your blessings and I have mine." And when we are trying desperately to heal from hurts that have grown deep in us, we need to find some way to accept the apology that we continually are asking for, even when the truth seems to be that we will never receive it.

In the midst of this examination and inventory of all our relationships, it is important that we not forget that we need to nurture and examine the relationship that we have with ourselves. This is ultimately what all of the other relationships echo and expose— who are we with ourselves.

Bottom line, we are being invited to choose to not let others be in charge of our sense of self. Only God has that "right" to influence our well-being—yes, this relationship with God is the primal and central relationship for each of us. And we know what God's stance is: God believes us all to be wonderful, indeed! Sometimes people will never understand or accept our own personal journey. And we will not always be able to understand theirs. That is OK. There is no rule that we have to understand these changing and divergent paths that we may be taking. It may not be the same for them. It may not be the same for us. But we need to choose life—for ourselves and, yes, for the other as well.

■ PROCESS

Questions for Reflection and Action
FOR INDIVIDUAL AND GROUP REFLECTION

Who are the primary people who are life-giving to me?

What relationships are changing? How are they changing?

How can I let go of the need to "be right" in the midst of conflictual relationships?

How can I let go when every sign seems to point toward that?

What are some new "strategies" for me to take on, in order to stay healthy in my relationships?

Song-Prayers

May We Not Conform
DAVID HAAS, GIA PUBLICATIONS
Digital MP3 Download available from www.giamusic.com: X-56605

Nothing Can Keep Us From God's Love
DAVID HAAS, GIA PUBLICATIONS
Digital MP3 Download available from www.giamusic.com: X-51712

SEVEN

Embrace brokenness; celebrate weakness

We have this treasure in clay pots so that the awesome power belongs to God and doesn't come from us. ◆ **2 CORINTHIANS 4:7**

If it's necessary to brag, I'll brag about my weaknesses.
◆ **2 CORINTHIANS 11:30**

I'm all right with weaknesses, insults, disasters, harassments, and stressful situations for the sake of Christ, because when I am weak, then I'm strong. ◆ **2 CORINTHIANS 12:10**

It takes a long time to move from power to weakness, from glib certitude to vulnerability, from meritocracy to pure grace...We ourselves grow through vulnerability and not through any need to posture, pose, or present. How clever of God! Now only the humble will ever find God...The egoic or unconverted self reads everything in terms of its own ascent, various attempts at spiritual achievement, the attaining of merits and rewards, climbing upward, performing for God, concocting my own worthiness game, and then pretending I am succeeding at it. It is all so futile and so unnecessary.
◆ **RICHARD ROHR, OFM; ADAPTED FROM** *Great Themes of Paul: Life as Participation*

As we grow older, we often feel that we do not have the same "stuff" anymore, that our skill-sets have diminished, or as we musicians say, that we are losing "our chops." Guess what? To a degree, this is most certainly true. There is no way that all of us can maintain forever the level of external abilities we may have enjoyed during our so-called "prime." They can't last forever!

But here is the thing. While our more familiar "chops" will at some point begin to wither (it will be different for everyone; there is no one tempo at which these things happen), the changes open up new doors. We will enter rooms where we will discover some "new" stuff, some new talents, some new insights, some new wisdom or gifts that we can offer. "Behold I make all things new!" is God's promise. And these "new things" will be more mature, more seasoned, and better tested, because there is some real life that we can bring to them.

When we sit in the reality of our weakness, we should cultivate some compassion for ourselves, even delight in this a little. We need to soften our view a bit and remember that we are not alone.

Our weakness and brokenness need not scare us. It need not be the source of so much worry. Remember the faith we proclaim when we gaze upon the cross, the central symbol of our faith. We believe in, follow, and walk with a naked, bruised, and vulnerable Jesus. We place all of our hopes in a beaten, abused, broken man who was shamed and brought low. Brokenness. Weakness. And holiness.

Our God is one who may sit very high, but this God also looks low, bending down and choosing to walk with us as *human*, in our most vulnerable state. Brokenness. Weakness. "When I am weak, then I am strong."

Do we have the courage to surrender our lives to one who knows us better than we know ourselves, the one who knows the deepest cries that stir in our hearts? Can we "get over ourselves" to rest in this most blessed promise: that we are not alone, that there is a plan (even though we may at this moment have no blessed idea what it might be), a path, and a restful place that we will one day discover and make our home?

In the end, the gift of being human, of really being alive, lies with what we choose to do with our pain. This is the "whole" and "holy" life. We can try to avoid it, stuff it, run from it, and escape it. But we cannot. What will we do with our pain? Celebrating weakness and brokenness allows us to cry inwardly and allows God to come in and befriend our pain and suffering. When we can honestly and courageously face our pain and brokenness, our beautiful selves will be more revealed to us and to the world. Then, God's glory, ironically, is more fully known. It will help us to remember who we are and who God really is. It will bring us closer to God, which in the end, is what we all so desperately seek.

But we cannot climb toward it or earn it or "accomplish" it. We need to surrender to it. This is faith. We all have a deep need as fragile and holy human beings to offer ourselves like a flute, a hole in which God's breath can enter and blow around a bit.

There is no way around it. Brokenness and weakness are part of the path to holiness. So let us be holy, then. Lying deep within our weakness is the depth of God's most awesome love. This is what Paul means when speaks about his "boast" in the cross (Galatians 6:14). To take up the cross is to rejoice in our pain, not in a masochistic way but because it means that we are *alive*. It is there where we find Christ more present than in any other way.

We need to have the courage to not walk away from our brokenness but move closer to it. When we do so, God will be there. May we keep practicing humility like we would practice our favorite instrument. Daily. In prayer. May we surrender our ongoing attempts to determine and control the path of our lives. May we stretch out and reach out not only with our hands but with our hearts. With all that we are. With all that we have. With all that we ache for. With all of the dreams that we dream. With all that we hold on to. May we able to give it all up.

We do not need to be afraid. Whatever fear we have, may it be, for us, a most precious and holy fear. This is the fear, the brokenness, and the weakness that can open up doors for us, leading us to an even more holy transformation.

■ PROCESS

Questions for Reflection and Action
FOR INDIVIDUAL AND GROUP REFLECTION

Can I identify the aspects of my life that seem to be diminishing?

How can I embrace weakness when every other voice and force that surrounds me seems to work against this?

What are some ways that I/we can befriend our brokenness?

How can I/we walk with others who are making this same journey?

Song-Prayers

In the Power of Christ
DAVID HAAS, GIA PUBLICATIONS
*Digital MP3 Download available
from www.giamusic.com: X-55608*

With You By My Side
DAVID HAAS, GIA PUBLICATIONS
*Digital MP3 Download available
from www.giamusic.com: X-73114*

EIGHT

Live "smaller"

*O Lord, my heart is not proud, nor haughty my eyes. I have not gone after
things too great, nor marvels beyond me.* • **PSALM 131:1, DH PARAPHRASE**

Where your treasure is, there your heart will be also. • **MATTHEW 6:21**

*We didn't bring anything into the world and so we can't take
anything out of it.* • **1 TIMOTHY 6:7**

Sing God a simple song: Lauda, laude...
• **STEPHEN SCHWARTZ AND LEONARD BERNSTEIN,** *Mass*

Living "smaller" means to try to remove not only the physical clut-
ter that may consume our surroundings but the things, thoughts,
voices, and other sources of stress that fill and are pushing at the
boundaries of our sanity. We not only accumulate physical stuff; we
accumulate thoughts, obsessions, and so many other things that
bruise our minds, our memories, and our attitudes.

As much as we may want to, we cannot have everything we want.
Nor should we.

But our minds and hearts rebel against this. We live in a culture
and time (especially in North America) where the need to "ascend"
surrounds us, consumes us, and holds an extraordinary amount of
power over us. The need to climb, to improve ourselves, to push

ourselves to excellence, to perfection, is not only encouraged but thrust upon us from every side. It is an obsession that is rewarded not only in our job environments but in family life and, yes, by ourselves to ourselves. It becomes the standard by which we hold and judge others.

We want to be successful. We want to make a difference. We want to make contributions that will be significant to the lives of others. We want to be well thought of in the things that we do. We feel that if we can accumulate more knowledge, read more books, take more classes, stretch our minds more, possess things not only of quality but in quantity, all this will increase who we are and what others think of us; it will improve how we see ourselves. We want to look in the mirror and like what we see. We want to be proud of who we are and what we have accomplished. We want others to be "proud" of us—our parents, our spouses and partners, our children, our friends and colleagues. We want to surround ourselves with nice things—not necessarily extravagant things, but things that give us comfort and increase our sense of well-being.

And whether we are aware of it or not, most of the time this accumulation help us to forget our vulnerability. The "stuff" and the "things" help us to escape being with ourselves, naked and true.

This *drive* to *strive*, to have and possess, so often becomes our way of not facing who we really are. It protects and enables a false self—a false way of looking at the world, at our relationships and, yes, a false way of accepting ourselves for who we are in God's eyes.

At the source of this is ego. It may not appear like arrogance or puffed out pride, but it's ego nevertheless. The ego somehow convinces us that we need to have things and surroundings that will protect us and give us a sense of well-being. The ego needs to be fed, and we feed it by this endless and addictive cycle of accumulation. Often when people reach old age, some of the wisdom needed to counter this begins to emerge. As we get older, we want to get rid of more and more "stuff" that we have accumulated; we have great projects to purge and give things away. We begin to realize that we do not need all of these things that we have been hanging on to. We ask ourselves, "Why have I kept this for all of these years?" This is part of the "falling-upward" that Fr. Richard Rohr speaks about. We spend the first half of our lives ascending, achieving, possessing, accumulating, and owning things. Fr. Henri Nouwen spoke often of the "upward mobility" that we spend so much of our lives seeking. The invitation is to consider, hopefully sooner than later, that perhaps this pattern that we all seem to live in is useless and futile. The way of Christ is to consider living more in the "middle" of things, and to live "smaller."

This is a call to humility. And humility is something we have to keep working at, something that we have to keep practicing, just like we practice playing a musical instrument. As a musician, if I let my skills go and stop practicing, like I did as a young student (believing that I had done enough of that, and so I could rest on my laurels), I will soon come to see that my fingers on the piano do not move with the same facility and skill any more. It becomes more and more of a struggle to get through a piece of music.

Well the same is true with humility. We have to keep at it. Practicing humility does not mean we walk around with our head low or that we have always self-deprecate and put ourselves down. That is not humility at all. We are called to live in the light and not keep the light hidden. But humility *does* mean this: that we daily— yes daily—recognize that without God we can do nothing. This is true holiness—to live each day, and every moment of that day, with the full knowledge and joy that everything we have and accomplish is because we lean on and walk with God every step of our lives. It is what St. Thérèse of Lisieux meant by following the "little way."

God is inviting us to consider having a "quality" of life, as opposed to a "quantity" of life. We are often like squirrels, gathering as many nuts as we can into our corners. After we have gathered them all, we often do not know what to do with them, and they can become more and more of a problem. As we grow older, we feel as though we have to say "yes" to everything, because we are afraid of no longer remaining relevant to others and the world. As our mental abilities shed a bit, our fears take over, and we end up feeling as though we may lose them altogether. "Gather ye rosebuds while ye may." We need to store up and to shore up in order to stay relevant and necessary to the world.

We spend so much time climbing up that it's hard to travel to a place that may seem behind us. To follow in the way of Jesus Christ is to allow wisdom to take hold of us and to follow the command to "give up your life." This is not personal martyrdom, but an intentional walk to seek out what our life really is about. When we do that, when we make our life a bit "smaller," we come closer to living as servants for others.

Can we fall in love with the simple things, the smaller things? Can we let go of the need to have everything in our lives have a profound impact? Can we let go of the addiction to being extraordinary? Let God be extraordinary. Let Christ be the Messiah. We are being invited to take on a new destiny that is much more important than our life accomplishments, much more than what we have produced.

We do not need to see this as "crashing." Just the opposite. There is a new vocation waiting for us. To do less, to be less, to "decrease" so that God's wonderful activity in our lives can "increase." St. Catherine of Siena said it this way: "You are rewarded not according to your work or your time, but according to the measure of your love." We need to create space for that love to explode. Our bowls have become too big, too deep to fill, to help us feel adequate. Let's find a smaller bowl.

Can we do just the ordinary and simple things? Because if we can do this, just a little better then we presently are, we will probably find out that we are very special indeed. And, yes, relevant—

now more than over. But not in the ways that we have thought before. Our lives do make a difference. Our contributions are the fact that we *are*—not what we have produced or accumulated. But we need to live "smaller" so we can see it more clearly.

Some pruning needs to take place. So we need to do a few things. Yes, we need to get rid of more and more of our "stuff," the things and possessions that often, actually, possess us. But it is more than just the material things, the surroundings that we can see, touch, taste, and feel. We need to also rid ourselves of the idea that we are in control of our lives. We need to renounce the things and forces around us that keep us from being humble enough to see that it is in living smaller that we can actually accomplish and do great things. And these "great things" are exactly that—they are tremendous.

To live smaller is not to be cursed. Just the opposite. It is to live in a more authentic and holy way—lavishly.

A simpler song will do very well.

■ PROCESS

Questions for Reflection and Action
FOR INDIVIDUAL AND GROUP REFLECTION

What in my life do I need to surrender?
How do I practice surrender?

How can I surrender the "drive to strive"?

How can I keep moving toward making my life "smaller" without feeling as though I am losing something?

Song-Prayer

Come Follow Me
DAVID HAAS, GIA PUBLICATIONS
Digital MP3 Download available
from www.giamusic.com: X-89605

NINE

Choose gratitude; be thankful

Give thanks in every situation. ◆ **I THESSALONIANS 5:18A**

I thank my God every time I mention you in my prayers. ◆ **PHILIPPIANS 1:3**

Be thankful people. ◆ **COLOSSIANS 3:15B**

If the only prayer I prayed today was 'thank you,' that would be enough.
MEISTER ECKHART

The most mature kind of prayer or, for that matter, the most grace- and miracle-filled spiritual life, always moves toward and revels in a stance of gratitude.

Yet for some reason being grateful and giving thanks—rejoicing in the good things, the good people, and the good things that they do—seems at times to frighten us, threaten us, and even cause great dis-ease.

But the gift and posture of gratitude will lead only to good things being produced in and from us. Being grateful and choosing thankfulness makes us just as vulnerable and intimate as falling in love or feeling hurt and broken. When we take the risk to be grate- ful, we are, then, in that very moment, choosing *not* to be filled with negativity. When we are grateful, jealousy begins to wither away, and with it the desire to cause harm to another. When we are grateful, we are not consumed with ourselves; we are not selfish. When we are grateful, our creative muse spins out some of the most beautiful things, and then we cannot help but share them with our sisters and brothers.

When we are grateful, we can truly give without conditions or expectations. Our giving then becomes lavish, because we are giving out of a sense of complete freedom. We have no need to "get something back." When we are grateful, the good things then become blessings, and we can receive them with an open heart and joyously celebrate them all.

When we are grateful, we can really accept—without reserve, embarrassment, or discomfort—that we are God's children and that we are loved beyond our wildest dreams.

When we wake each day, may we choose to give thanks to God for the simplest and yet very profound things: "I am awake. I can see, feel, touch, and move," or whatever those most basic things are for us.

Whenever we create or accomplish or complete something, we can stop for a moment and give thanks. When someone offers us praise, even when we may not feel at that moment that we have done anything very praiseworthy, we can give thanks. When we have some quality time with a friend, we can give thanks. When healing takes place in a troubled relationship, we can give thanks. When forgiveness is shared, we can give thanks. Even when we try something and fall short or even fail, we can give thanks. When we think of our spouses, partners, friends, and family, and our spiritual guides and mentors, we can give thanks. Give thanks as Paul does: "I thank my God every time I remember you" (Philippians 1:3, NRSV).

Let us think of the marvelous friends we have, and let us give thanks. They all contribute to the quality and sacredness of our lives. Many of us have friends that go way back in time whom we do not see often at all, but when we do see them, it is like picking up where we left off. Some of these people we may not have seen for years, but we know deep down that they are present in our lives. What a gift! Give thanks for that.

We have others in our lives who truly listen to us and honor who we are; they have taught us much and still continue to do so. Give thanks! We have people in our lives who make us laugh until our sides ache and hurt, and those who stand by us in the darkest and loneliest of times. Give thanks! And give thanks for others, for their lives, for what they have accomplished. And yes, give thanks for the "good times" and "good things" that may have drifted away. Especially be thankful for these things.

We could go on and on, if we really think about it. Not everyone may be as equally blessed, and we know that.

Choose gratitude over bitterness.
Choose thankfulness over resentment.
Choose happiness over anger.
Choose promise over reneging.
Choose smiling over grimacing.
Choose goodness over evil.

So, let us all take a moment right now. Call to mind some gratitude. Give thanks!

■ PROCESS

Questions for Reflection and Action
FOR INDIVIDUAL AND GROUP REFLECTION

What are the simple everyday things in my life that I am grateful for?

What are the situations in my life where gratitude seems to be absent?

What might be a daily pattern of prayer and attitude that I can begin to practice to become a more grateful and thankful person?

Do I take time in my life to write down or bring to mind the things in my life that are blessings to me?

Song-Prayers

The Name of God DAVID HAAS, GIA PUBLICATIONS
Digital MP3 Download available from www.giamusic.com: X-26514

Throughout All Time DAVID HAAS, GIA PUBLICATIONS
Digital MP3 Download available from www.giamusic.com: X-80502

Every Time I Remember You
DAVID HAAS, GIA PUBLICATIONS
Digital MP3 Download available from www.giamusic.com: X-97010

TEN

Stay creative

I have set life and death, blessing and curse before you. Now choose life.
• DEUTERONOMY 30:19

We are the clay, and you are our potter. All of us are the work of your hand.
• ISAIAH 64:8B

We are God's accomplishment, created in Christ Jesus to do good things.
God planned for these good things to be the way that we live our lives.
• EPHESIANS 2:10

Don't neglect the spiritual gift in you that was given through prophecy when
the elders laid hands on you. Practice these things, and live by them so that
your progress will be visible to all. Focus on working on your own
development and on what you teach. • I TIMOTHY 4:14–16A

God's cause is the only concern of our hearts.
BLESSED THERESA GERHARDINGER, SSND

To remain creative is to choose life. And vice versa. When we choose
life, creativity not only opens up, it can pour out so fast that we
sometimes cannot keep up with it.

Choose life! God is here. This is God's wish and gift for all of us.
God is present in each of us. Nothing more is being asked of us than

to recognize this. When we can be attentive to this presence, we can move through our days celebrating it. If we are open, it can and will fill us to the brim. And then the light that we feel against our face and feel burning in our hearts can bring the heat that can empower us to light up the world. This is creativity.

For Johann Sebastian Bach, every creative utterance of his was a "giving back" to the Holy One, to God. Remember the mantra that was offered in Practice 5? "God's cause is the only concern of our hearts." For Bach, God's cause was always at the forefront of everything. On every manuscript of every composition he completed, he attached the announcement: "Soli Deo Gloria" (to God alone be the glory). God's cause.

But the "creative" process and charism is not just about what we may compose, write, sculpt, paint, craft, cook, or otherwise produce. Keeping creative is to remain vibrant and alive in how we relate to others, in the way we treat one another. It is about God's cause. When we routinely drive by a homeless person who is looking for a few dollars to survive, let us remember God's cause. When we become stubborn in our constant need to be right and for the other person to be wrong—let's choose differently; let's be creative. Let's remember God's cause.

The one addiction that we all have is the addiction to our need to be *right,* the addiction to our own thinking. It is as if to say, "in my humble and correct opinion..." If our creative process is going to be holy and filled with integrity (in other words, of God), perhaps we need to consider that there is a way, a lens, a source of wisdom other than our own.

Here is the ultimate criterion for evaluating whether or not we are being creative and whether not what we are creating is worthy and noble. Is it of God? If God in some way is not being glorified or being announced in some way (it does not have to be overt), then it is not of God. Sometimes when we are trying to be creative, to accomplish or finish something, we can become distracted from God's cause. These distractions actually become the road-block. I know of friends who work in the corporate world, but they still ask themselves, "Am I doing God's work here?"

As a composer, I am called to help announce "God's cause." But the music is not the only vehicle for making that cause known. God's cause is found in the homeless person that we drive by on the street when we are usually in a hurry to get some place. God's cause is found in the sick, the dying, and those who seem to suffer endlessly. God's cause is found in the young people who are fearful and anxious about their future.

Conversely, God's cause is not to be found in the feeding of our egos (which is hard for creative people to face!), but in the feeding of the hungry. God's cause is not found when we merely talk and sing about the poor; it is found in the very poor themselves. God's cause must sing beyond the song; it must bring about beauty beyond the painting itself; it must move and grow beyond the movement of the gift of the skilled dancer; it must bring the poetry to life beyond the metaphors and images of the poem itself. When our creative output points to and nurtures such things, then the creative work is of God. Then we can truly say: "Soli Deo Gloria."

What are the things that truly sabotage our creativity? Every time a gifted cantor I know approaches the ambo to lead the responsorial psalm on Sunday, she repeats this mantra: "Not me, but you... not me, but you." A mantra like this need not be limited to the more "churchy" ministries; it should be part of everything we do.

Being and remaining creative is to trust, as Thomas Merton would say, the "brightness of the Holy Spirit" that is doing its work in us. We were born by and into this brightness. As we age in this brightness, certain aspects of our creativity will diminish, but the brightness endures. We never "retire" from being alive in the Spirit of God.

Let's stay bright. Let us remain focused on God's cause. Let's keep choosing life. Let's keep the "Soli Deo Gloria" in front of us, surrounding us. Let's be truly creative and be the vehicle for the beautiful, unexplainable, and very holy things of God.

■ PROCESS

Questions for Reflection and Action
FOR INDIVIDUAL AND GROUP REFLECTION

What are the outward expressions of my creativity? What are the things in my life that others recognize in me, that are creative and generative, but that I have a difficult time recognizing myself?

What are the roadblocks that bruise the "muse" in my life?

How can I still serve, create, and share but do so in a new and different creative way?

Song-Prayers

We Choose Life
DAVID HAAS, GIA PUBLICATIONS
*Digital MP3 Download available
from www.giamusic.com: X-51709*

Creating God
DAVID HAAS, GIA PUBLICATIONS
*Digital MP3 Download available
from www.giamusic.com: X-21307*

ELEVEN

Remain connected; nurture community

How good and pleasant it is when God's people live together in unity!
• **PSALM 133:1, NIV**

....

The community of believers was one in heart and mind. None of them would say, "This is mine!" about any of their possessions, but held everything in common. The apostles continued to bear powerful witness to the resurrection of the Lord Jesus, and an abundance of grace was at work among them all. There were no needy persons among them...
• **ACTS 4:32–34A**

....

Don't do anything for selfish purposes, but with humility think of others as better than yourselves. Instead of each person watching out for their own good, watch out for what is better for others. • **PHILIPPIANS 2:3–4**

....

Community is first of all a quality of the heart. It grows from the spiritual knowledge that we are alive not for ourselves but for one another. Community is the fruit of our capacity to make the interests of others more important than our own (see Philippians 2:4). The question, therefore, is not "How can we make community?" but "How can we develop and nurture giving hearts?" • **HENRI NOUWEN,** *Bread for the Journey*

I have a friend of many years who, when I first met him at a con-
ference, shared with me that he lived in an intentional Christian
community. About a year or so later, I traveled to visit him. After
he picked me up at the airport, he took me to his two-bedroom
apartment. I said to him, "I thought you lived in community." He
laughingly responded with, "Well, yeah, community is great. The
only bad thing about community is all of the people."

Can you relate? All of us—even if we are introverts—have a
basic need and desire to feel connected in some way with others.
"Belonging" is very important, perhaps even critical, for the human soul. Research has shown that people's desire to join a church
or faith community is grounded not so much in deepening their
relationship with a power greater than themselves (God) but in
the need to belong to a group that shares values, beliefs, and a
common desire for meaning. Although we long for it, we also
know how difficult community is, how challenging it is to trust
and invest in relationships with others.

We know how difficult it is simply to belong to a volunteer
committee, how difficult it can be to make decisions together because of the various and complex personalities around the table.
Working on a team, whether it be at work or as a volunteer, can
be maddening because people find it difficult to work together
and come to a consensus. Compromise is difficult. In the end, we
often throw our hands up in the air and simply want to "make it
easier and do it myself."

So there is a "yin and yang" here. We want to be connected, especially spiritually, but we also experience how difficult that is. We want
to learn, grow, and be challenged, but we also want to be part of a
church or group of people who think the same way we do. We love
people, but life often seems easier when we just go onward by ourselves. We want to receive the Body of Christ in the bread and wine,
but we find it difficult to "receive" the gift of the "body of Christ" in
each other—the communal witness of God truly being with us.

Many people, when expressing their deepest convictions about their Christian faith, will speak about having a "personal relationship with Jesus Christ." Others will express their need to go to church so they can "be alone with God." Isn't this interesting? Some people will get into their cars and drive twenty minutes or more to enter a church building containing 500 people or more, so they can be "alone with God." For some Catholics, adoration of the Blessed Sacrament has become more important than going to communion. As important as personal prayer is, and as important as it is that we nurture our individual relationship with God, that is not what the Eucharistic liturgy is about. Liturgy basically means the "common work of the people." We are good about going to church, but we are not always so good about *being Church together*.

The same is true not just in terms of our public worship and devotional life. When we speak about our faith and our journey with God, some of us will say something like, "my religion, my faith is between God and me, nobody else." We are living in an age where diversity—especially religious diversity—not only scares us but often leads us to the belief that we actually have to demonize the other and, yes, stop them.

All of this results in a great contradiction. We want to feel connected, but we also, intentionally and unintentionally, choose to isolate.

Meanwhile, the ongoing, relentless and uncompromising voice of God is speaking to us:

You will be my people, and I will be your God. (Jeremiah 30:22)

There it is. And it does not just appear in Jeremiah; all through the Hebrew Scriptures, God proclaims the relationship between the Holy One and human beings. No wiggling around or out of it. We are invited, called, and even commanded at times to be connected with God and to understand, accept, and embrace the fact that this connection requires us to be connected to each other. As Christians, we call this the "Mystical Body of Christ."

The presence of Christ transcends our admiration and nostalgia for the historical person of Jesus. "Christ" means that Jesus transcends his historical and human life. "Christ" means that this holy presence is here all around us, in the breathing and living human beings that are with us in this world. This holy presence is not primarily "present" and known in things, in inanimate objects, in *nouns*. No, this Christ is present to us as *verbs*! People loving, breathing, living, hurting, being wounded, and being wonderful. People who are like us and people who are not—just plain folks! This is the amazing and awesome reality about our God. Our God is not, as the popular song from years ago tried to say, "watching us from a distance." God is active, engaged, and stirring right here. Here!

Yes, we believe Jesus is present in the tabernacle, in the consecrated bread and wine. Yes, we believe that Christ is alive when we proclaim, listen to, and preach the word of God. Yes, we believe that God is present in the beauty of creation—on the earth (even though we do not treat it very well), in the stars, and in the heavens. God is present in all of these things.

However, we often forget and need to rediscover that God is so profoundly present in human beings! We find God in each other. This is the wonderful and, at the same time, maddening truth. We need to allow the scales to fall from our eyes and to be consumed by the blazing flash of light that celebrates this holy presence in every person. Every single human being, those we know and those we do not know, those we love and those we find difficult to love, those who believe differently than we do, those we do not understand, those we find offensive—everyone is a vessel for God.

This is why community is important and why we are called to stay connected. It's why hospitality and welcome are so key to our holiness, both individually and collectively.

A young adult once shared with me, "If I were not present at church on Sunday over a period of time, would I be missed?" Everything in our hearts should respond with a resounding "Yes!" You, my young friend, not only are missed, but when you are not here, we are less. When we are connected in a holy way with others, we feel this deeply. Community celebrates our need for each other and that we become better people when we are alongside each other.

Community. Connection. Not only at church, or at "Church"! But everywhere, in every season, in every circumstance, in every setting. For the life of the world.

◼ PROCESS

Questions for Reflection and Action
FOR INDIVIDUAL AND GROUP REFLECTION

*Who are the various circles of community in my life?
Is there a primary one?*

*What are the things that others are looking for when seeking out
connections with people? What am I looking and hoping for when
I join a group or a church community or choose other circles of
connection?*

*How can I be a more nurturing presence to others in the various
groups and communities to which I belong?*

Song-Prayers

One Heart, One Mind DAVID HAAS, GIA PUBLICATIONS
Digital MP3 Download available from www.giamusic.com: X-95102

Table Song DAVID HAAS, GIA PUBLICATIONS
Digital MP3 Download available from www.giamusic.com: X-80610

All Is Ready DAVID HAAS, GIA PUBLICATIONS
Digital MP3 Download available from www.giamusic.com: X-63104

TWELVE

Be a prophet; be a blessing

Contribute to the needs of God's people, and welcome strangers into your home. Bless people who harass you—bless and don't curse them.

• **ROMANS 12:13–14**

....

Pursue love, and use your ambition to try to get spiritual gifts but especially so that you might prophesy. This is because those who speak in a tongue don't speak to people but to God; no one understands it—they speak mysteries by the Spirit. Those who prophesy speak to people, building them up, and giving them encouragement and comfort. People who speak in a tongue build up themselves; those who prophesy build up the church.

• **I CORINTHIANS 14:1–4**

....

Don't pay back evil for evil or insult for insult. Instead, give blessing in return. You were called to do this so that you might inherit a blessing.

• **I PETER 3:9**

....

To give someone a blessing is the most significant affirmation we can offer.

• **HENRI NOUWEN,** *Life of the Beloved*

Everything points to this: Be a prophet; be a blessing
It is about moving outward in everything we do, with everything that we are, and with all that we hope for. It is at the highest
calling of what it means to live wholly and holy. Let this be our
ongoing litany of intent and discipleship—of being prophets and
blessing-givers:

Our hands—moving toward the poor.

Our minds—moving toward those aching
for insight and wisdom.

Our feet—moving toward walking with,
alongside a fellow traveler.

Our ears—moving toward attentive listening to the anxious.

Our tears—moving toward crying with the sorrowful.

Our presence—moving toward being there with the lonely.

Our focus—moving toward helping another
who is distracted.

Our gifts—moving toward the building
and lifting up of the community.

Our eagerness—moving toward deepening
hospitality and welcome.

Our wisdom—moving toward guiding those who are lost.

Our strength and protection—moving toward caring
for the fears of others.

Our memories—moving toward keeping
the stories of others alive.

Our generosity—moving toward feeding
and nurturing those who are groping for hope.

Our compassion—moving toward expanding our hearts.

Our mercy—moving toward deepening and acting
with forgiveness, healing, and attentiveness.

Our hearts—moving toward harvesting the love of God.

Our blessing—moving toward being living signs
of mission and holiness.

Do not pull away from seeing yourself as a prophet. That image
frightens us; it seems too "high" for many of us, way beyond our
reach. We do not see ourselves as prophets because we do not think
we are holy or profound enough. That's because we really do not
understand the biblical understanding of who a prophet is. A
prophet is not a seer or a fortune-teller who knows the future. A
prophet does not have an inside line to God.

Biblically speaking, a prophet is simply (though it is not a simple
calling by any means) a "spokesperson for God." That is our call, a
gift given to us in baptism. We are to speak for God, to announce
and radiate God's presence, and, as Paul says, "to build up the
church." We speak for God, because we speak for God's people, to
"give encouragement and comfort."

And if we are children of God, our call is also to be a "blessing." To bless someone is "to speak well" of them. In God's eyes, we are all "blessings," and every single one of us deserves blessings from each other. You are a blessing. I am a blessing. We are God's beloved children, and that means we are called to speak and radiate that blessing to everyone we encounter.

To understand ourselves as a blessing to God and others, we need to seek out God's heart and keep the light of God shining brightly within us. We are not defined by our personality traits or even less so by any "disorders" that we may perceive ourselves to have or that others may want to thrust upon us. Even when we fail, we are God's child, God's blessing. We are all blessings. We carry God inside of us.

We need to rid ourselves more and more of the notion that we are stained with "original sin" and focus more on the fact that we are God's "original blessing." We are God's unique and wonderful idea. You and I: precious, unique, gifted. It is hard to accept, isn't it? There are so many voices and forces that stir in us that say just the opposite.

But God would disagree. Most passionately so.

We have to move through the din of the fog and accept that we are God's marvelous blessing. When we do this, we are freed of shame. We are capable of glory and weakness, a blend that is not a contradiction in terms, but an expression and reality of God's movement in our lives. There is wonder in us. And, yes, there is brokenness in us. They are both part and parcel of a most beautiful gift.

This gift is not just for ourselves. This "chosen-ness" is how God sees everyone. If God can see this wonder in everyone, then we are seriously called to bless, name, and proclaim this "blessing" in ourselves *and* in each other. In this "zone" of blessedness we see God's lavish heart. We see wholeness and holiness.

So first, take some moments to look in the mirror and see yourselves as a blessing; and then be that blessing to yourself. Celebrate it. Sing it. Be a blessing with your heart, and with the entirety of your life. When we realize this, we can realize covenants of love with God, each other, and ourselves, achieving the deepest communion with the God who loves us.

■ PROCESS

Questions for Reflection and Action
FOR INDIVIDUAL AND GROUP REFLECTION

Who are the prophets—whether from the Bible or other places—that have inspired and influenced my life?

What are the qualities of these prophets?

How can I be more of a source of blessing to the many people in my life?

How can my entire life "be a blessing" to the world?

Song-Prayers

Be A Blessing DAVID HAAS, GIA PUBLICATIONS
Digital MP3 Download available from www.giamusic.com: X-95920

To Be A Servant DAVID HAAS, GIA PUBLICATIONS
Digital MP3 Download available from www.giamusic.com: X-80308

The Servant Song
RICHARD GILLARD, ARR. DAVID HAAS, GIA PUBLICATIONS
Digital MP3 Download available from www.giamusic.com: X-71607

A FINAL REFLECTION

Holiness is breath—not death.

Holiness is movement—not paralysis.

Holiness is rejoicing—not hopeless lament.

Holiness is always about creating beginnings—
   not anticipating endings.

Holiness is hope that never disappoints—not promises never kept.

Holiness is bursting rivers—not flooding sewers.

Holiness is mending—not ripping apart.

Holiness is about being—not fading.

Holiness is gracious light—not the cruel darkness.

Holiness is the hoped-for paradise—
   not the fear and gloom of hell.

Holiness is healing hands—not the bruising sword.

Holiness is an expanding heart—not the shrinking spirit.

Holiness is the song of love—not the dirge of hate and division.

Holiness is the consoling softness—not the shaming, hard edge.

Holiness is restoration—not destruction.

Holiness is forgiveness—not the haunting of judgment
   or the threat of revenge.

Holiness is the endless outpouring of mercy—
   not the harshness of hopelessness.

Holiness is the beauty of life itself—not the ugly lurking of decay.

Holiness is everlasting goodness—not the pathetic path of evil.

Holiness is the garden of Easter—not the desert
   of horror and grave.

The journey toward holiness

is where and when you realize

that your life is not your own,

while at the same time,

you come to discover that you surrender

to God's path and love for you;

you are more "you" than you have ever been before.

The journey toward holiness (we never arrive there completely)

is the place

when you can, for however long possible,

carve your way inside

the unexplainable love of God,

and discover just how large your life can be.

David Haas *is from Eagan, Minnesota, and is recognized as one of the preeminent liturgical composers in the English-speaking world. He has published and recorded more than 50 original collections of music for sung prayer. In addition, he is active as a workshop and retreat leader, author, concert performer and recording artist. David was nominated for a Grammy Award in 1991, and in 2015 received an Honorary Doctorate in Humane Letters from the University of Portland in Oregon.*